MISTY TWISTY KNOT

Thinking Cap – The Power of Your Thoughts

By Stephanie Brinkley Wellon

Overview

Thinking Cap – The Power of Your Thoughts, offers strategies to assist youth with recognizing and disrupting unhealthy thought patterns. Faulty, disruptive or irrational thought patterns can be interrupted and replaced with healthy thinking patterns when identified and addressed with appropriate interventions.

Parents, educators and loved ones play a vital role in the shaping of our children. Therefore, we must begin the process, early on, of nurturing healthy thoughts, minds and teaching our children how to process their feelings.

This unique tool, extends the conversation to understanding how thoughts, emotions and behaviors, impacts our overall emotional and mental well–being.

Dedication

In Loving Memory of my father

Alfred Lee Brinkley
May 26, 1945 - February 11, 2019.

In loving memory of my mother

Sandra Ruth Brinkley

April 9, 1948 – June 6, 2021

In loving memory of my grandmother

China Mae Neal

March 12, 1926 - November 8, 2021

In loving memory of my uncle

Jaime Brinkley,

April 4, 1951 - May 8, 2022

You are forever in my heart

To my husband Gary and children: Kenneth, Gary Jr., LaGarass, LaGarren & Devin and my beautiful grandchildren: Jordan, Bre'yana, Riley and Gabriel: The true wind beneath my wings.

God Children: La'Quantany, Crystal and Marcellus, I love you.

Hello everyone! It's me, Misty Twisty Knot. I am so glad to be with you again. I have missed you a lot. I'm more relaxed nowadays and feeling much better. I'm still seeing my counselor and I have made a lot of progress. So what do you think about my new green cap? I call it my thinking cap because it has been quite helpful with getting me to think through things. There have been times when things have gotten tough and I did not feel my best, but I'm managing.

MEMORY TEST!

Hmmm…Let's see what you remember from my first book *Misty Twisty Knot-Understanding Emotions and Behaviors Associated With Anxiety.*

1.   Was I forgetful?
2.   Did I worry a lot?
3.   How many days of school did I miss because of Ang-zi-e'-tee (Anxiety)?
4.   What was my name before I was called Misty Twisty Knot?
5.   What is the name of my best friend?
6.   Name two things that I did to get rid of anxiety.

HOW IT WORKS:

Situation: The process begins with a situation.

Thoughts + Feelings =Behavior

1)   We Think
2)   We Feel
3)   We Behave

Thoughts influence Feelings. Feelings influence Behavior.

We Feel, We Think and We Behave

In the world of Misty Twisty Knot, thoughts are either crooked or straight. If they are crooked, they are unable to help you in anyway. However, if they are straight, you are well on your way to success.

Note: The causes of disruptive, faulty or negative thinking patterns, can be traced back to negative childhood experiences, failed relationships with significant parental figures or harmful interactions later in life. Child abuse, abandonment, and domestic violence are just a few of the factors that can contribute to thought disorders.

When left alone, and without access to viable resources, children may become self-reliant to make the best of what has been handed to them. Consequently, their worldview, beliefs and interpretations of situations are shaped from negative experiences; thereby, creating disruptive thinking patterns.

When Misty wears her thinking cap, she makes good choices and almost always does the right thing repeatedly.

Misty believes that she has more positive thoughts because of the green energy and power that comes from wearing her green thinking cap.

When Misty uses her thinking index finger and taps three times: 1, 2 and 3; while repeating the words: think, think, think, Misty can't help but have positive thinking, which is now done so easily.

When Misty takes off her thinking cap, it does not help her in any way. Misty just feels sad, mad, angry and frustrated for most of the day.

CROOKED THOUGHT

Just because it happened then, it doesn't mean that it will happen again.

I'm going to die just like my grandpa did.

I can do it.

My mom will never get out of jail.

Something bad is going to happen.

I can't do it.

No one is perfect.

My best is enough.

I can do it right all the time

I'm not bad at anything

Something is going to happen.

I have to do it right all the time

I have to do it right all the time

I have to do it right all the time

I don't have to do it right all the time

If I don't check the door, something bad will happen.

I can!

Nobody likes me.

I can't do anything right.

Daddy is going to die in the war.

He's going to hurt me again.

Others have been hurt but that's all I know

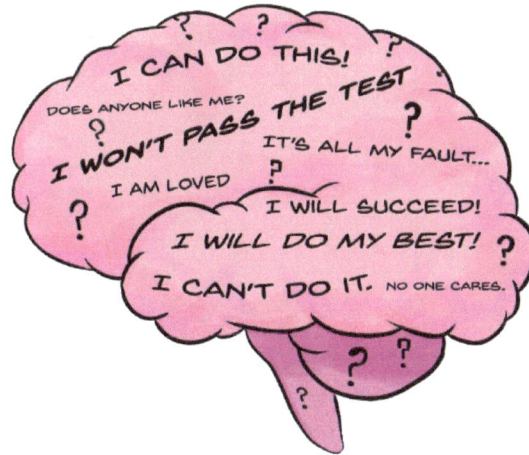

Just as there are many languages in the world, there are also many thoughts. Thoughts become language that takes place in the brain. Did you know that you could have more than a thousand thoughts a day?

How many thoughts have you had today? What are you thinking about right now?

Our thoughts can be crooked or straight. Straight thoughts will leave you feeling okay. Crooked thoughts will not leave you feeling that way.

Exercise:

Remember that in the world of Misty Twisty Knot, thoughts are either crooked or straight. If they are crooked, they are unable to help you in anyway, but if they are straight thoughts, you are on your way to success.

1)   Take a look at the picture of the brain on this page.

2)   Now name the crooked thoughts and then name the straight thoughts located in the brain.

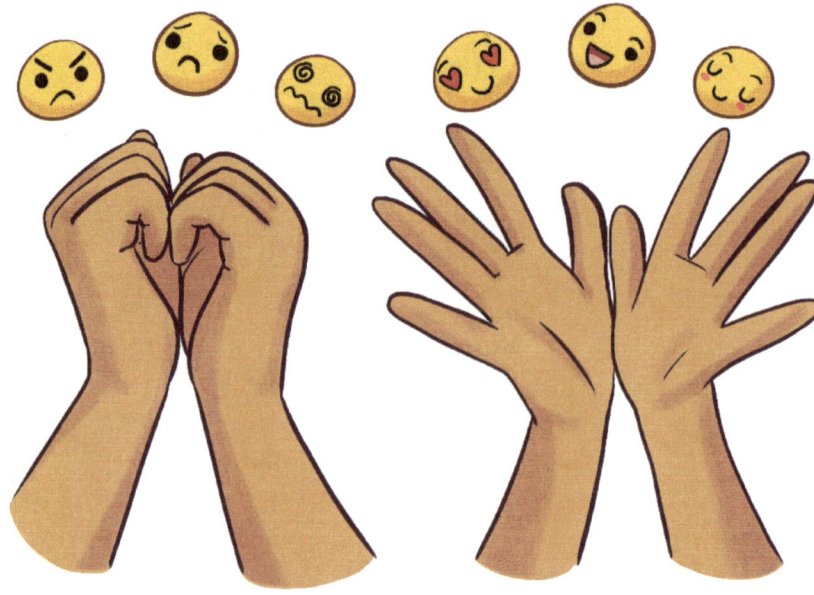

Thought + Feeling =Behavior

Teaching Note: Feelings -Emotions can be pleasant and at other times, they can feel painful or overwhelming. Thoughts and feelings standing separate from one another have less energy and are not a powerful force. For a feeling to have any power it has to connect with a thought. If a feeling is attached to a straight thought, you're okay, but if it's connected to a crooked thought, you are simply not thinking and behaving the correct way.

Feelings are emotions. Feelings can be felt in the heart and in other parts of the body. We can also experience a sensation, which is also a physical experience.

Example (1):   When you feel love in your heart you can also feel butterflies or warmth in your body. Love is the feeling; the butterflies and warmth are the sensations.

Example (2):   You feel nervous or afraid and also feel butterflies in your stomach or very hot sensations in your body.

Example (3):   You feel hungry and your stomach begins to growl.

Point to Remember: A feeling and sensation are ways that your body communicates or alerts you to knowing how you are feeling and responding to a situation.

Exercise:

Try naming the six (6) feelings as shown on the feeling faces at the top of page seven (7), and as many sensations that you experience with each feeling.

Pledge to become a positive thinker like Misty

I Pledge To Think About What I Am Thinking
I Pledge To Think Before I Act
I Can Think The Right Way!

Learn to think about what you are thinking and then it will be much easier to think before you act. Remember to use your thinking index finger: Tap three times 1, 2 and 3; while repeating the words: think, think, think.

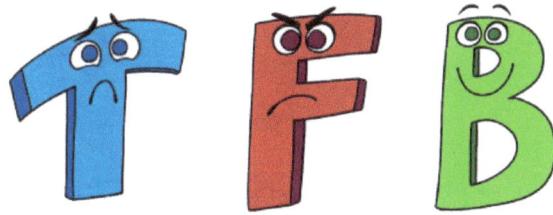

Thoughts + Feelings= Behavior.

Who we are and who we will become will happen because of our Self-Concept (thoughts of self) and self -esteem (feeling's about self).

Name three (3) thoughts that you have about yourself.

Examples:
I am smart
I am fun to be around
Nobody likes me

Name three (3) feelings that you feel when you think about the thought you named.

Examples:
Happy
Confident
Disappointed/Sad

Name how you might behave when you combine the thought and the feeling that you named together.

Examples:
Thumbs Up

Hanging out with my friends at the movie
Staying to myself

Identifying Thoughts

- I will pass my test
- I can't do it
- My best is good enough
- I'm good enough
- Something bad is going to happen
- I am going to get in trouble
- No one is perfect
- Just because it happened then, it does not mean that it will happen again
- I can
- I will
- There will be another shooting
- Daddy is going to die in the war
- If I study hard, I will have a better chance of passing my test

Exercise Set Up:

Explain that we are going to review and practice identifying thoughts. Ask students to review the list of thoughts from above.

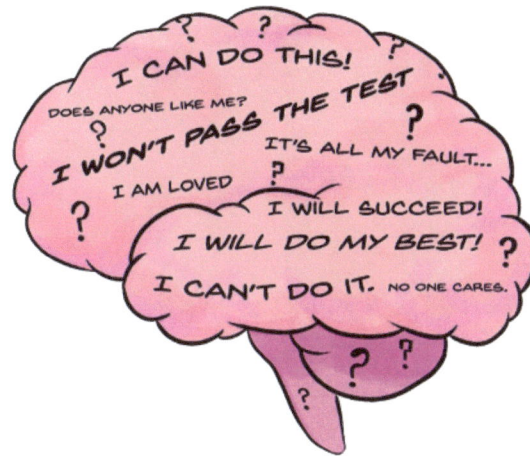

1) **First Thoughts:** This activity can be completed individually or in a group setting. Have the student(s) to record their first thoughts for one minute. First thoughts are thoughts that automatically pop up. If completing individually, remind students that they have the option to share or not to share their thoughts with the group.

2) For any thoughts that you have chosen, name whether they are crooked or straight.

Remember: Our thoughts can be crooked or straight. Straight thoughts will leave you feeling okay. Crooked thoughts will not leave you feeling that way.

Materials needed: timer, pencil/pen, paper or journal, marker and a large sheet of paper for recording group responses. Non-judgmental attitude required.

Identifying Feelings

- Excited
- Frustrated
- Proud
- Afraid
- Nervous
- Calm
- Comfortable
- Confident
- Courage
- Worried
- Anxious
- Optimistic

Exercise Set Up:

Explain that we are now going to review and practice identifying feelings. Ask students to review the list of feelings from above. Ask if anyone has any questions or comments about any of the feelings listed above.

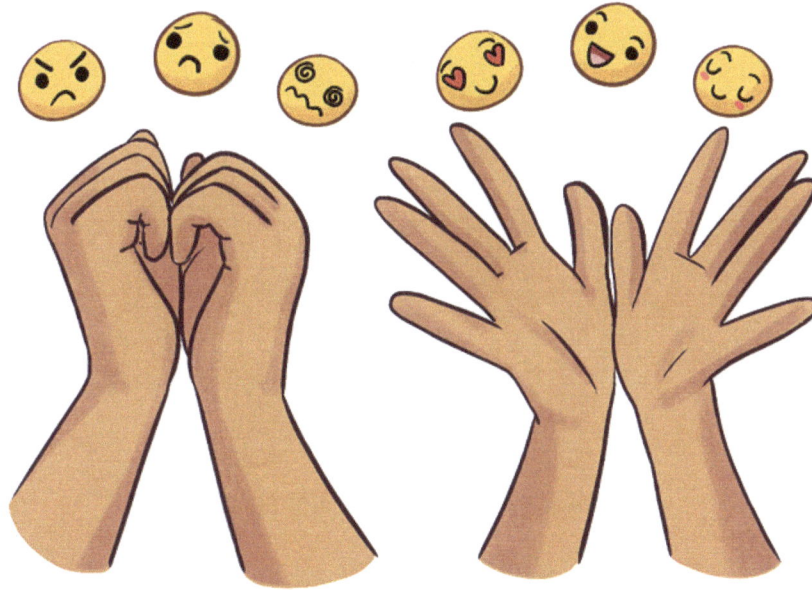

1) **Naming Feelings:** This activity can be completed individually or in a group setting. Have student(s) record their feelings for one minute. Students are asked to name feelings that they are experiencing in the moment along with any sensations. If completing individually, remind students that they have the option to share or not to share their feelings with the group.

Materials needed: timer, pencil/pen, paper or journal, marker and a large sheet of paper for recording group responses. Non-judgmental attitude required.

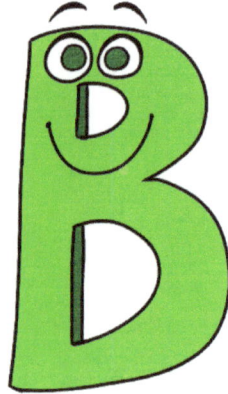

Identifying Behaviors

- Smiling
- Not auditioning for the school play
- Auditioning for the school chorus after not making it the first time
- Sitting with peers who are dressed differently from you
- Choosing not to go on the class trip because you have to fly on an airplane
- I don't tell the truth about something that I did that was wrong
- I try again even though I made a mistake
- I take a flight
- I take on a challenge
- I take on a challenge again and again
- I speak negatively all the time
- I watch the nightly news every night to hear about fighting overseas
- I complete my homework as soon as I arrive home from school

Exercise Set Up:

Explain that we are now going to review and practice identifying behaviors. A behavior is how you act or what I would see you doing in response to a thought or feeling. Ask students to review the list of behaviors from the previous page. Ask if anyone has questions or wants to comment about any of the behaviors listed above.

1) **My Behaviors:** This activity can be completed individually or in a group setting. Ask students to think about behaviors that they engage in everyday and write them down for one minute. Have students think about routine behaviors for prompting, e.g., getting out of bed and brushing their teeth. If completing individually, remind students that they have the option to share or not to share their responses with the group.

Materials needed: timer, pencil/pen, paper or journal, marker and a large sheet of paper for recording group responses. Non-judgmental attitude required.

Activity:

Decide whether either of the following is a Thought, Feeling or Behavior:

- ✔ I might embarrass myself
- ✔ Nervous
- ✔ Happy
- ✔ Walking
- ✔ Talking
- ✔ I'm not going to school today
- ✔ Brushing my teeth
- ✔ Making my bed
- ✔ I enjoy going to school
- ✔ I can do this

Faulty Thinking Example:

Thinking Cap and Green Energy Strategies required.

(T) I'm not going to attend the class trip because something bad is going to happen.

(F) Nervous.

(B) You chose not to go on the class trip because you have to fly on a plane.

Question: Is your thinking cap on or off? Are your thoughts crooked or straight?

16

Hint#: Where's the Proof? What evidence do I have that something bad is going to happen?

Hint#: Truth. Something bad did happen but I have no evidence or proof that it will happen again.

Remember that in the world of Misty Twisty Knot, thoughts are either crooked or straight. If they are crooked then, we must hurry to learn how to think the right way.

~THINKING CAPS REQUIRED BEYOND THIS POINT~

Green Energy in Full Force

1) Learn to think about what you are thinking and then it will be much easier to think before you act. Remember to use your thinking index finger: Tap three times 1, 2 and 3; while repeating the words: think, think, think.

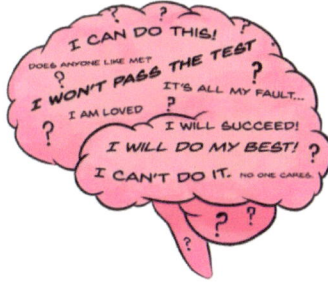

2)	Name your thought

Ask yourself, Where's the Proof? Search for the proof that your thought is true. If you don't find any proof, you are on your way.

Strategies for Identifying and Disrupting Faulty Thinking

3)	Tell yourself the truth about your thought. Ask yourself: "Is my thought true, false or I Don't Know?"

4)	Take a deep breath in through your nose, hold for the count of one, exhale slowly and then be at ease. Repeat three (3) times.

5)	Imagine yourself breathing slowly in through your nose and out through your mouth. Repeat (3) times.

✔	Play the game: Keeping Up With Your Breath. Simply focus on keeping up with your inhale and your exhale while breathing in through your nose and out through your mouth. Don't get ahead of your breath or lag behind. Your goal is to stay with your breath; to slow that sprinter like breathing down. Slow, slow and easy. Slow it down.

✔	**Grounding:** Wherever you are (sitting or standing), take a pause and remind yourself of your name_____, the time of day_____, your location_____ and the purpose of you being at the location_____.

✔ Misty Twisty Knot learned to talk about her thoughts and feelings openly and honestly. Misty Twisty Knot learned that writing her thoughts and feelings down by **journaling** was the most incredible thing.

Strategies for Identifying and Disrupting Faulty Thinking

✔ **FIVE (5) Good Senses:** Utilize all five (5) senses to become mindful of all that you are experiencing in your environment and body:

  o **SIGHT**: Look around and pay attention to what you see.

  o **SMELL:** While inhaling (breathing in through your nose), pay attention to any aroma or fragrance that you had not been aware of before.

  o **HEARING:** Close your eyes and just listen for sounds in your environment.

  o **TASTE:** Move your tongue around in your mouth while engaging your taste buds and identify what you taste.

  o **TOUCH:** Notice the temperature in the room. Feel your shirt collar around your neck and your belt around your waist.

✔ Repeat the following: I am calm, I am relaxed and I am safe. Believe It!

✔ Pledge to become a positive thinker like Misty Twisty Knot:

I Pledge To Think About What I Am Thinking.
I Pledge To Think Before I Act.
I Can Think The Right Way!

✔ Remember that yesterday is gone, tomorrow is not here yet, so be careful not to allow yesterday and what you think will happen on tomorrow cause you to miss the great things that could happen today.

Let's Practice What We Have Learned!

Putting It All Together

Instructions: Review the lists of Thoughts, Feelings and Behaviors listed on pages 10, 12, and 14. Refer to the TFB's that you have written down individually or shared in your group and complete the following:

✔ Practice identifying which is a Thought, Feeling or Behavior

✔ On a blank sheet of paper write the words Thoughts, Feelings and Behavior in three separate columns

✔ For each Thought, Feeling or Behavior that you have named, place the TFB in the correct column.

✔ Determine if your thoughts are crooked or straight.

✔ If crooked, put on your green thinking cap and employ green energy strategies to help you think the right way. (Refer to pages 18-21)

Misty Twisty Knot Pledge!

No More Worries
No More Fears
Talk It Out, Don't Act It Out
You Can Talk About What Is Bothering You

Positive Thinker Pledge!

I Pledge To Think About What I Am Thinking.
I Pledge To Think Before I Act.
I Can Think The Right Way
As Long As I Have On My Green Thinking Cap!

~The Case of Misty Twisty Knots Best Friend Andy~

When Misty Twisty Knot felt anxiety, she named a few trusted adults that she could talk to about her feelings and thoughts. There was her mommy and daddy, her grandma and granddaddy but there was also her best friend Andy.

~THINKING CAP Strategies Required~

Green Energy Sources Are In Full Force

Instructions:

On your own or in your groups of three, help me to support my best friend Andy who is sitting in the principals' office. This situation is really bothering me.

✔ Name some thoughts that Andy might be thinking. (Page 10)

✔ Name some feelings and sensations that Andy might be experiencing. (Page 12)

✔ Name some behaviors that Andy might engage in when he has the thoughts and feelings that you name. (Page 14)

24

✔ Discuss what thoughts you might have about what is happening in this scene with my best friend Andy?

✔ Where is Andy's green thinking cap? (Find it on page 24)

Refer to pages 18-21. Put your Green Thinking CAP on - Use Green Energy Strategies

Remember: *Our thoughts can be crooked or straight. Straight thoughts will leave you feeling okay. Crooked thoughts will not leave you feeling that way.*

Turn to page (26) to learn about the truth and what was really happening with Andy!

The Truth About the Case of Andy!

Andy's principal called him to the office to inform him that he would be receiving an award for most improved grade in his reading class. Andy's principal had been assigned the responsibility of coordinating the awards banquet as Andy's teacher, who normally coordinates the banquet, had been assigned to another task.

Truth: Andy had taken off his thinking cap, placed it beside him and had resorted to faulty thinking because he had not done well in reading in the past.

Remember that yesterday is gone and tomorrow is not here yet. Be careful not to allow yesterday and what you think will happen tomorrow to cause you to miss the great things that could happen today.

Always remember to wear your green thinking cap. Think about what you are thinking and to think before you act.

Congratulations!

When you find yourself feeling tense, tight and tied up like a knot, it's time to re-focus and think about your thoughts. You will find that in most situations you have resorted back to distorted, faulty and disruptive thinking patterns.

By the way, did I forget to mention another source of powerful green energy? The key is to feed your brain with all of the good stuff that comes from eating your green, leafy vegetables. Remember to THINK, THINK, THINK and be at ease.

Your Thoughts Have Power!

See you soon!

Misty Twisty Knot